MIDWEST SMALL TOWN COOK
by
Bruce Carlson

Hearts 'N Tummies Cookbook Co.

3544 Blakslee St.
Wever, IA 52658
800-571-2665

©1994 Bruce Carlson
ISBN: 1-57166-006-2

SO, WHAT'S SO SPECIAL ABOUT MIDWEST SMALL TOWN COOKIN'?

Maybe it's the folks chatting over the back yard fence, trading recipes or parts of recipes. Maybe everybody's makin' note of whose dish ends up empty first at the church social, and folks gotta do some really high-powered cookin' outta self defense. Maybe it's somethin' else, I dunno. But, I do know that there's cookin' goin' on out in the little towns of the Midwest that's second to none.

SALADS

3

SMALL TOWN SALADS

Cauliflower Pea Salad........................13
Cucumber Salad 9
Green Salad-Slaw 5
Hot German Potato Salad................11
Orange Tapioca Salad 12
Pennsylvania Dutch Coleslaw...........16
Pineapple Salad 10
Potato Salad..................................7
Sauerkraut Slaw 8
Shoestring Potato Salad 6
Spinach Salad................................17
Spring Salad 14
Strawberry Salad 15

GREEN SALAD · SLAW

1 head cauliflower
  (broken into flowerettes)
1 small can shrimp
1 C. cooked rice
½ C. chopped green pepper

12 sliced stuffed green olives
1 C. Miracle Whip
2 T. lemon juice
Salt & pepper, to taste
1 small onion (diced)

Gently toss cauliflower, shrimp, rice, onion, green pepper and olives. Mix Miracle Whip, lemon juice, salt and pepper; add to first mixture. Refrigerate overnight before serving. (All ingredients may be used in whatever proportions you desire.)

SHOESTRING POTATO SALAD

1 C. celery (diced)
2 boiled eggs (cut-up)
1 C. chicken, turkey, tuna or ham
1 C. grated carrots

1 small onion (diced or minced)
1 C. Miracle Whip
Salt, pepper & garlic powder, to taste
1 small can shoestring potatoes

Mix all ingredients, except potatoes. Add potatoes when ready to serve.

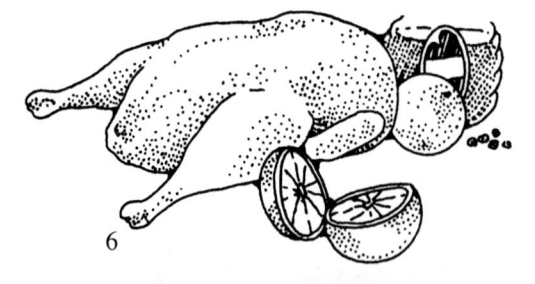

6

POTATO SALAD

10 potatoes
   (boil with skin & peel when warm)
6 eggs (boiled)

4 sweet pickles
1 medium onion (diced)

SAUCE:
1⅓ C. Miracle Whip
1½ tsp. salt
½ tsp. pepper
1 T. vinegar

½ tsp. celery seed
1 T. sugar
½ C. milk

Cut-up potatoes, eggs, pickles and onion. Add sauce and mix well. Sprinkle with paprika.

SAUERKRAUT SLAW

1 can kraut (32 oz.) (undrained)
1¼ C. sugar or 1 C. honey
1 C. chopped onion

1 C. chopped celery
1 C. chopped green pepper
⅓ C. pimento

Mix all ingredients thoroughly and keep in refrigerator 2 days before using to blend flavors. The result is a very tasty salad. (Smaller cans of kraut may be used, then use half of other ingredients.)

CUCUMBER SALAD

Pour 1 ½ to 1 ¾ C. boiling water over a 3 oz. pkg. of lime gelatin and stir until dissolved. Let stand until it begins to set. Add 1 C. ground or grated cucumber to the above along with ½ C. mayonnaise, 1 T. grated onion and salt & pepper, to taste. Mix well and pour into molds. Serve on lettuce with mayonnaise. Serves 6 to 8

PINEAPPLE SALAD

1 large can crushed pineapple
1½ C. miniature marshmallows
½ C. nuts (chopped)

1 large container Cool Whip
Drain pineapple & use juice
   in dressing

COMBINE FOR DRESSING:
1 C. pineapple juice
½ C. sugar

2 T. cornstarch
1 egg (beaten)

Cook over medium heat until thick (watch carefully). Add pineapple while still hot. Cool completely. Add Cool Whip, marshmallows and nuts. Pour into a large salad bowl and chill. Just before serving fold in cut bananas, if desired.

HOT GERMAN POTATO SALAD

3 lbs. peeled potatoes
6 slices bacon
¾ C. chopped onion
2 T. flour
2 T. sugar

2 tsp. salt
½ tsp. celery seed
Dash of pepper
¾ C. water
⅓ C. vinegar

Cook potatoes in boiling salted water until done; drain and set set aside. In big skillet, fry bacon crisp, remove and drian on paper towel. In bacon drippings fry onions until golden. Stir in flour, sugar, salt, celery seed and pepper. Cook over low heat, stirring until bubbly. Remove from heat and stir in water and vinegar. Heat to boiling, stirring constantly; boil for 1 minute. Crumble bacon and thinly sliced potatoes. Stir into mixture and heat thoroughly, stirring lightly.

ORANGE TAPIOCA SALAD

1 (3 oz.) pkg. tapioca pudding
1 (3 oz.) pkg. orange Jello
1 (3 oz.) pkg. vanilla pudding
1 can mandrain oranges

1 small can pineapple tidbits
2 bananas
2 C. Cool Whip

Combine Jello, puddings, 2½ C. hot water and juices from fruit. Cook until thick and bubbly, stirring constantly. Add fruits and then cool. Add Cool Whip and chill until set. Makes a large bowl and will keep a few days.

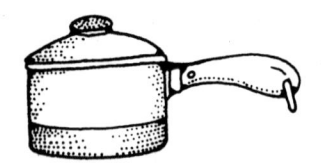

CAULIFLOWER PEA SALAD

1 head of cauliflower
  (broke into pieces)
1 pkg. frozen peas (cooked & drained)
1 C. chopped celery
2 T. finely chopped onion

¼ C. milk
1 C. mayonnaise
1½ tsp. Hidden Valley Ranch
  dressing mix

Place vegetables in bowl. Combine mayonnaise, dressing mix and milk. Pour over vegetables and mix well. This is better if made a day ahead.

SPRING SALAD

Mix 1 (3 oz.) pkg. lemon or lime Jello according to directions. Cool until partially set. Whip and add 1 C. Cool Whip, 1 C. crushed pineapple (drained), ¼ C. fine chopped celery and ¼ C. nutmeats; put in small Pyrex pan. If you double recipe, use 1 box lemon and 1 box of lime.

STAWBERRY SALAD

1 (6 oz.) pkg. strawberry Jello 10 oz. pkg. frozen strawberries
2 C. boiling water   1 C. applesauce

Add boiling water to Jello and stir. Fold in strawberries and applesauce. Pour in 9x9-inch pan.

PENNSYLVANIA DUTCH COLESLAW

½ C. whipping cream (whipped)
2 T. sugar
3 T. cider vinegar

½ tsp. celery seed
¼ tsp. salt
5 C. shredded red or green cabbage

In large bowl, fold sugar, vinegar, celery seed and salt into cream. Toss lightly with cabbage. Cover and chill. Refrigerate leftovers. Makes 6 to 8 servings.

SPINACH SALAD

Fresh spinach (washed & torn for 8)
Sliced oranges (2 medium)
Baco chips
Grated Monterey Jack cheese

1-2 chopped hard-boiled eggs
(optional)
Chopped green onion or minced onion
(optional)

DRESSING: (Enough for 2 Salads)
1 C. vinegar
2 C. sugar
1 tsp. dry mustard

1 tsp. celery seed
1 tsp. paprika
¼ C. grated onion (optional)

Boil for 2 minutes, then add ¾ C. vegetable oil. Cool and pour over salad.

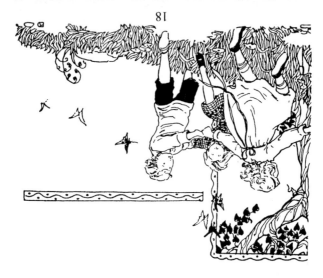

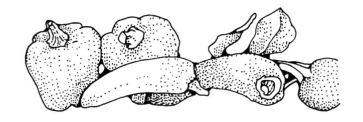

VEGGIES

SMALL TOWN VEGGIES

SWISS VEGETABLE MEDLEY

1 (16 oz.) bag frozen broccoli, carrots
  and cauliflower
  (thawed and drained)
1 (10¾ oz.) can cream of mushroom
  soup
1 C. (4 oz.) shredded Swiss cheese

⅓ C. sour cream
¼ tsp. black pepper
1 jar chopped pimento
  (drained, optional)
1 can Durkee French fried onions

Combine vegetables, soup, ½ C. cheese, sour cream, pepper, pimento and ½ can French fried onions. Pour into a 1-qt. casserole. Bake, covered, at 350° for 30 minutes. Top with remaining cheese and onions. Bake, uncovered, 5 minutes longer.

For Microwave: Prepare as above. Cook, covered on High 8 minutes; turn halfway through. Top with remaining cheese and onions. Cook uncovered, on High 1 minute or until cheese melts. Serves 6.

CREAMED BROCCOLI

1 T. oleo   ½ chopped onion
1 pkg. broccoli

Cook these together and let stand.

1 can creamed chicken soup   1 C. minute rice (add dry)
¼ C. evaporated milk   1 small jar Cheese Whiz or
1 C. water   1 can cheddar cheese soup

Cook second mixture together until thick. Add to first mixture. Put in 2-qt. casserole and in 350° oven for 20 minutes.

SCALLOPED CORN

1 can whole kernel corn
1 can cream style corn
½ C. butter

8 oz. sour cream
1 pkg. Jiffy corn bread mix

Mix and bake 45 minutes or so in square bake dish.

LIMA BEAN CASSEROLE

3 (10 oz. ea.) pkgs. frozen lima beans   ½ tsp. salt
5 slices bacon (diced & fried)   1 ¾ C. milk
3 T. bacon drippings   1 pkg. dry Italian salad mix
3 T. flour   ⅔ C. shredded American cheese

Cook beans in boiling salted water until done and drain. While beans are cooking, fry bacon and remove from grease. To bacon drippings add flour and salt, then stir in the milk. Cook until mixture thickens and add dressing mix. Add beans to this mixture. Pour half of bean mixture into 8x12-inch pan or casserole. Sprinkle with bacon pieces, then cheese and pour the remaining bean mixture into casserole. Bake in moderate oven for 25 to 30 minutes. This is an excellent vegetable casserole to take to a potluck supper.

SNACKS

SMALL TOWN SNACKS

SANDWICH BITES

1 lb. hamburger   1 lb. sausage
1 lb. Velveeta cheese   1 loaf cocktail rye bread

Brown hamburger and sausage. Drain off most of the grease. Add Velveeta cheese and stir until melted. Place mixture by spoonfuls on small cocktail bread slices. Place on cookie sheet and place under broiler. Broil until bubbly. Can freeze and broil as needed.

SHRIMP SPREAD

8 oz. pkg. Phil. cream cheese
Garlic powder
Onion powder or dry onion
2 tsp. lemon juice
2 tsp. Worcestershire sauce

3 oz. chili sauce
3 oz. cocktail sauces
   (comes in a bottle like ketchup)
1 can tiny shrimp
Parsley flakes

Mix cream cheese, garlic powder, onion, lemon juice and Worcestershire sauce together; spread on bottom of serving plate. On top cheese mixture spread chili sauce, cocktail sauce, tiny shrimp and parsley flakes. Serve with crackers or chips.

STRAWBERRY SOUP

¾ lb. strawberries
1 ½ C. water
¾ C. sherry
¼ C. tapioca
¾ C. sugar

¼ C. sherry
¾ lb. strawberries
2 C. whipped cream
8 oz. yogurt

Wash and puree fruit. Combine 1 ½ C. of water, ¾ C. sherry, ¼ C. tapioca and sugar. Bring to a boil; cool and add remaining ingredients. Serve with a fruit plate.

CAULIFLOWER DIP

2 C. Hellman's mayonnaise
1 small grated onion

2 tsp. Worcestershire sauce
½ tsp. garlic salt

Mix together and use as a dip for cauliflower.

AUNTIE CAROL'S VEGETABLE DIP

1 pt. Hellmans mayonnaise
2 T. onion flakes
4 tsp. soy sauce

½ tsp. ginger
2 T. milk
1 tsp. vinegar

Mix together and chill.

RAW VEGETABLE DIP

1 C. sour cream   1 pkg. Knorr's leek soup

Combine the two till well mixed. Chill overnight. Serve with celery, carrots, raw cauliflower and green pepper strips, etc. Also good with crackers or potato chips. Excellent on baked potatoes.

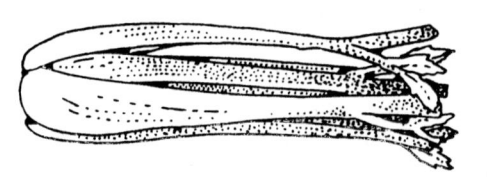

RAW APPLE DIP

8 oz. lite-whipped cream cheese   ¼ C. white sugar
¾ C. brown sugar   ½ tsp. vanilla

Mix well. Very good on raw apple slices.

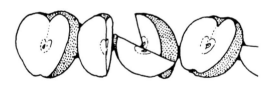

SOUP

SMALL TOWN SOUP

HOMEMADE POTATO SOUP

6-8 potatoes (cut in bite-size pieces)
2 onions (chopped)
4 chicken bouillon cubes or 4 tsp.
  instant bouillon

5-6 C. water
Salt and pepper
½ C. butter (1 stick)
1 (13 oz.) can evaporated milk
  (last)

Cook all above ingredients until potatoes are tender. Last ½ hour, add the can of evaporated milk.

COMPANY CHILI

3 T. vegetable oil
2 cloves garlic (minced)
2 large onions (chopped)
2 lbs. ground beef (chuck)
1 tsp. salt
¼ tsp. tabasco sauce
1/8 tsp. black pepper

¼ tsp. chili powder
½ tsp. ground cumin
2 (6 oz. ea.) cans tomato paste
2 (16 oz. ea.) cans tomatoes
  (drained)
2 (15 oz. ea.) cans red kidney beans
  (drained)

Heat oil and add garlic and onion; saute. Add ground meat and salt; brown meat.
Add rest of ingredients and cover; simmer for 1 hour. Add kidney beans and simmer for 15 minutes more.

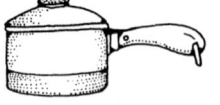

TURKEY (CHICKEN) WILD RICE SOUP

2 (10¾ oz.) cans cond. chicken broth
2 C. water
½ C. uncooked wild rice (rinsed)
½ C. finely chopped green onions
½ C. oleo or butter
¾ C. flour
½ tsp. salt
¼ tsp. poultry seasoning
1/8 tsp. pepper
2 C. Half & Half
1½ C. cubed cooked turkey or chicken
8 slices bacon (crisp & crumbled)
1 T. chopped pimento
2 or 3 T. dry sherry or white wine, if desired

Combine chicken broth and water, wild rice and onion. Bring to boil, reduce heat, cover and simmer for about 35 minutes or until rice is tender. Melt oleo and stir in flour, salt and seasonings. Cook, stirring constantly until smooth and bubbly. Gradually stir in Half & Half. Cook until slightly thickened, stirring constantly. Slowly add Half & Half into rice mixture. Again stirring constantly. Add remaining ingredients. Heat gently, stirring often. Do Not Boil!

COOKIES
& BARS

SMALL TOWN COOKIES & BARS

GINGER COOKIES

1 C. sugar
1 C. shortening
½ tsp. salt
1 egg
½ C. strong molasses (Brer Rabbit)

½ C. boiling water
1 tsp. soda
1 tsp. cinnamon
½ tsp. ginger
Flour to roll

Set in refrigerator overnight. Roll out next day and bake at 400° for 8 to 10 minutes.

ICE BOX COOKIES

1 C. brown sugar
1 C. white sugar
1 C. white Crisco
2 eggs
1 tsp. soda

1 tsp. cinnamon
1 tsp. baking powder
1 C. chopped walnuts
2½ C. flour

Cream sugars and Crisco; add eggs, soda, baking powder, cinnamon, chopped walnuts and flour. Dough will be stiff. Form into 3 loaves and chill or freeze. To bake, slice into ¼-inch or thinner slices and bake at 350°.

OATMEAL CRISPIES

1 C. shortening	1½ C. flour
1 C. white sugar	1 tsp. salt
1 C. brown sugar	1 tsp. soda
2 eggs	3 C. oatmeal
1 tsp. vanilla	½ C. nuts

Cream together shortening, sugars, eggs and vanilla. Sift together flour, salt and soda; add to sugar, eggs and shortening mixture. Mix in oatmeal and nuts. Make into rolls and wrap in waxed paper; put in refrigerator overnight. Slice ½-inch slices. Bake on cookie sheet at 375° for 10 to 12 minutes.

SUGAR COOKIES

1 C. sugar
1 C. butter
1 egg
1 tsp. vanilla

2½ C. flour
1 tsp. soda
1 tsp. cream of tartar

Mix all ingredients together and roll in balls; then roll in granulated sugar. Press on top with bottom of glass. Bake at 350° for 8 to 10 minutes.

GINGER SNAPS

1 C. shortening
1 C. sugar
1 egg
¼ C. molasses
2 C. flour

½ tsp. salt
2 tsp. soda
½ tsp. ginger
1 tsp. cinnamon
¼ tsp. cloves

Cream shortening and sugar. Add egg and molasses. Mix in dry ingredients. Make into balls and roll in sugar. Bake at 375° for 10 minutes.

PECAN BALLS

1 C. shortening
½ C. powdered sugar
2 C. flour

¾ C. nutmeats
1 tsp. vanilla

Mix together and roll in balls. Bake at 300° for ½ hour. When done, roll in powdered sugar.

48

PEANUT BUTTER COOKIES

2½ C. flour
1 C. peanut butter
1 C. brown sugar
1 C. shortening

1½ tsp. baking soda
1 tsp. vanilla or lemon extract
Raisins, chocolate chips or
    coconut

Mix flour with peanut butter, brown sugar, shortenings and flavoring. Refrigerate until solid then roll into balls. Press down with a fork. Add raisins, chocolate chips or coconut, if desired. Keeps for a long time.

APPLE BARS

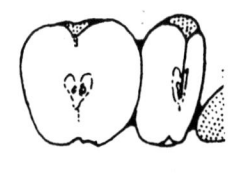

2½ C. flour
¼ tsp. salt
1 C. shortening
1 egg yolk
Milk

1 C. crushed corn flakes
4 large apples (sliced)
1 C. sugar
1 tsp. cinnamon

Add salt to flour and cut in shortening like pie crust. Beat yolk and add enough milk to egg yolk to make ⅔ cup. Add to dough mixture. Roll out ½ of dough and put in 10x15-inch pan. Cover dough with corn flakes, then with apple slices and sprinkle with sugar and cinnamon mixture over top. Roll out rest of dough and spread over top. Make cuts in top to let out steam. Beat egg white until stiff and brush over top. Bake at 350° for 1 hour. While still warm, frost with 1 C. powdered sugar, 1 T. water and 1 tsp. vanilla.

TOFFEE COOKIES

1 C. butter	2 C. flour
1 C. brown sugar	½ tsp. vanilla
1 egg yolk	¼ tsp. salt

TOPPING:
8 small Hershey bars   ½ C. nuts

Cream butter and brown sugar until light. Stir in egg yolk, then add remaining ingredients and mix well. Spread out in thin layer on cookie sheet. Make dough thickness of English toffee candy, about 3/16 of an inch. Bake at 350° for 25 minues. Remove cookies from oven and lay on candy bars. Let met and spread evenly over cookies. Sprinkle with chopped nuts and cut into small squares.

DATE NUT BALLS

½ C. margarine
¾ C. sugar
1 (8 oz.) pkg. chopped dates

2½ C. Rice Krispies
1 C. chopped pecans
Coconut

Bring margarine, sugar and dates to a boil and cook 3 minutes, stirring constantly. Remove from heat. Stir in Rice Krispies and pecans. Cool to touch. Shape into 1-inch balls and roll in coconut. Makes about 4 dozen.

SKILLET COOKIES

2 eggs
1 C. sugar
1½ C. chopped dates
1 tsp. vanilla

2½ C. Rice Krispies
½ C. chopped nuts
Coconut

Beat eggs and add sugar and dates. Cook until it collects in center of skillet; stirring most of the time. Remove from heat and add Rice Krispies and nuts. Roll into small balls and then roll in coconut.

APPLESAUCE BROWNIES

½ C. butter
2 sq. chocolate or 2 T. cocoa
1 C. sugar
2 well-beaten eggs
½ C. applesauce

1 C. flour
½ tsp. soda
½ tsp. salt
1 tsp. vanilla
½ C. nuts

Melt butter and chocolate together. Blend in sugar and and remaining ingredients. Bake at 350° for 40 minutes. Frost or use powdered sugar.

BUTTERSCOTCH BARS

4 C. oatmeal
1 C. brown sugar
1 C. melted butter

1 (12 oz.) pkg. butterscotch chips
¾ C. peanut butter

Mix first 3 ingredients and spread in 9½x13-inch cake pan. Bake at 350° for 12 minutes. Do not overbake. Melt the next 2 ingredients in a small pan, stirring constantly. Spread over first layer. (Setting-up time can be reduced by refrigerating for a short while.)

GRAHAM CRACKER BROWNIES

2 C. (about ⅓ lb.) graham cracker (crumbs)
1 (14 oz.) can Borden's sweetened cond. milk
1 (6 oz.) pkg. chocolate chips
Nuts as desired

Mix and pour into a 7x11-inch pan which has been greased. Bake at 325° for 35 minutes.

CHOCOLATE CAKE BROWNIES

¼ C. butter
1 C. sugar
2 eggs (unbeaten)
1 tsp. vanilla
2 sq. chocolate (melted)

½ C. milk
1 C. flour
½ tsp. baking powder
Dash of salt
Nutmeats

Mix all together and bake at 350°.

KRAFT CARAMEL BARS

2 C. oatmeal
1½ C. brown sugar
1 tsp. soda

1½ C. melted margarine
2 C. flour

Mix and put ½ in 9x13-inch pan. Bake at 350° for 10 minutes. Melt 50 caramels in milk to thin. Pour over baked crust. Pour 1½ C. chocolate chips over caramel sauce. Sprinkle remaining dough over all. Bake at 350° for 15 minutes more. Cut while warm, then go back through.

BROWNIES

2 C. sugar
4 eggs
1 tsp. vanilla
1½ C. flour

1 C. oleo
4 T. cocoa
¾ tsp. baking powder
Dash of salt

Cream sugar and oleo. Beat in eggs, 1 at a time. Add cocoa, vanilla and dry ingredients. Bake at 350° for about 25 minutes. May frost with powdered sugar frosting.

CHOCOLATE CHIP BARS

1 C. shortening or oleo
1 C. granulated sugar
½ C. brown sugar
2 eggs
2 tsp. vanilla

1 tsp. salt
¾ C. chocolate chips
2 C. sifted flour
1 tsp. soda
½ C. nuts (optional)

Beat oleo, sugar, brown sugar and eggs until fluffy. Add remaining ingredients and spread in ungreased cookie pan. DO NOT OVERBAKE. Bars will look done around edges and puffy in the middle when done, but will fall when taken out and cooled. Cut while warm. Bake at 375° for 13 to 15 minutes. Serves 24.

CARAMEL RIBBON BARS

1 pkg. yellow cake mix
½ C. chopped walnuts
⅔ C. evaporated milk
¼ C. butter or oleo (melted)

½ C. semi-sweet chocolate chips
  (optional)
½ C. Smuckers caramel topping

In mixing bowl combine dry cake mix and walnuts. Stir in evaporated milk and melted butter. Spread half of cake mixture in 9x13-inch pan. Bake at 350° for 10 minutes. Remove and sprinkle chocolate chips over hot crust. Drizzle with caramel topping. Drop remaining cake mixture by spoonfuls over all. Bake for 20 to 25 minutes more. Cool on wire rack and cut into squares.

FRUIT CAKE SQUARES

6 T. butter
1½ C. graham cracker crumbs
1 C. angel shredded coconut
2 C. mixed candied fruit (cut-up & mix pineapple and red & green cherries)

1 C. chopped dates (sprinkle flour on them)
1 C. chopped nuts
1 can sweetened condensed milk

In a 15½x10½x1-inch jelly roll pan melt butter. Sprinkle on crumbs evenly. (Tap sides of pan to get crumbs even.) Sprinkle on coconut. Scatter candied fruit over coconut. Scatter floured dates and then nuts over mixture. Press lightly with hands to level in pan. Pour milk evenly on top. Bake at 350° for 25 to 30 minutes. Cool and cut in squares.

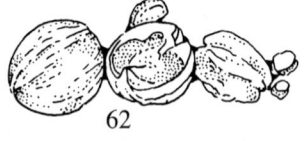

FUDGE-NUT BARS

1 (12 oz.) pkg. chocolate chips
1 C. sweetened condensed milk
2 T. butter
½ tsp. salt
1 C. chopped walnuts
2 tsp. vanilla
2½ C. flour

1 tsp. soda
1 tsp. salt
1 C. butter
2 C. firmly packed brown sugar
2 unbeaten eggs
2 tsp. vanilla
3 C. oatmeal

Melt chips, milk, butter and salt over hot water. Remove from heat and add walnuts and 2 tsp. vanilla; set aside. Sift flour, soda and salt. Cream butter and gradually add brown sugar. Add unbeaten eggs and 2 tsp. vanilla. Blend well. Stir in the dry ingredients and 3 C. of oatmeal. Press ⅔ of mixture in greased 9x13-inch pan. Spread with chocolate filling. Crumble remaining mixture over filling. Sprinkle with nuts. Bake at 350° for 25 to 30 minutes.

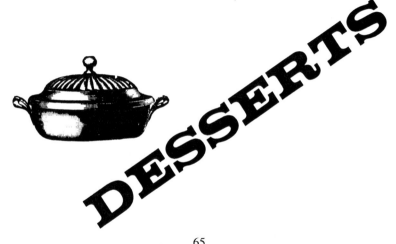

DESSERTS

SMALL TOWN DESSERTS

COCONUT PUDDING DESSERT

CRUST:
1 C. flour
¼ C. brown sugar
1 c. coconut
1 small pkg. slivered almonds

FILLING:
3 C. milk
2 pkgs. instant vanilla pudding*
1 (8 oz.) Cool Whip

(*Can use about any flavor.) For Crust: Mix all ingredients together and put into a 9x13-inch pan. Slice 1 stick oleo over the top. Bake in 350° oven stirring every 10 minutes until mixture is brown. For Filling: Mix pudding and milk until thick. Fold in whipped cream. Spread over the crust. Save some of the crumbs for the top. Refrigerate.

MRS. HOWARD'S CAKE

1 stick butter or margarine
1 C. flour
¾ C. crushed dry roasted peanuts
¼ C. peanut butter
1 C. powdered sugar

1 (8 oz.) pkg. cream cheese
2 (12 oz. ea.) containers Cool Whip
1 small instant chocolate pudding
1 small instant vanilla pudding
2¾ C. milk

Mix first 3 ingredients and put in 9x13-inch pan. Bake at 350° for 20 minutes. Mix peanut butter, powdered sugar, cream cheese and one container of Cool Whip until fluffy. Put on first layer. Mix chocolate and vanilla puddings and milk together. Put on second layer; let set. Spread remaining Cool Whip on top. Sprinkle with crushed dry roasted peanuts.

CLOUDS AT SUNRISE

6 egg whites
¾ tsp. cream of tartar
2 C. sugar
2 C. (about 45) crushed soda crackers

¾ C. chopped nuts
2 tsp. vanilla
2 C. whipped cream or Cool Whip
1 (21 oz.) can cherry pie filling

Preheat oven to 350°. Beat egg whites until frothy; add cream of tartar, then gradually add sugar. Beat until stiff. Fold in crushed crackers, nuts and vanilla. Spread in a well buttered 9x13-inch pan. Bake at 350° for 25 minutes. Cool on rack. Spread Cool Whip over top and spoon pie filling over whipped cream. Chill several hours or overnight before serving.

APPLE-MALLOW CRISP

4 ½ C. sliced apples
2 T. sugar
1 tsp. cinnamon
¼ tsp. nutmeg
2 tsp. lemon juice

8 marshmallows (quartered)
½ C. flour
¼ C. brown sugar (firmly packed)
½ tsp. salt
¼ C. butter or oleo

Combine apples, sugar, cinnamon, nutmeg, lemon juice and ¾ of the marshmallows. Butter a 1 ½-qt. baking dish. Spread apple mixture in dish in even layers. Combine flour, brown sugar and salt. Cut in butter until mixture is crumbly. Sprinkle over top of apples in baking dish. Dot with reserved marshmallows. Bake in 350° oven for 30-40 minutes until apples are tender and top crisp.

CHERRY OR APPLE PIZZA

1½ C. flour
⅓ C. shortening
2 T. butter or oleo
¾ tsp. salt
3-5 T. milk

1 C. brown sugar
½ C. butter
1 C. coconut
1 can pie filling

Mix the flour, shortening, butter, salt and milk as you would pie dough. Roll out to fit a cookie sheet. Mix together brown sugar, ½ C. butter and coconut. Sprinkle ⅔ over crust. Spread on the can of pie filling and sprinkle on remaining topping. Also, you can save some of the crust back and make a lattice top. Bake at 350°.

CHERRY DESSERT

1 (20 oz.) can crushed pineapple
1 can cherry pie filling
1 large white or yellow cake mix

1 stick margarine
½ C. nuts or coconut

Put pineapple evenly in a 9x13-inch pan. Spoon cherry pie filling over and spread. Sprinkle dry cake mix over cherry filling. Slice margarine thinly over entire cake. Sprinkle with nuts or coconut and bake at 350° for 50 minutes.

BLACK RASPBERRY DELIGHT

1 pt. black raspberry ice cream (soft)
1 pkg. instant vanilla pudding
1 envelope Knox gelatin

1 C. milk
Vanilla wafers
Cool Whip

Beat together first 4 ingredients. Pour over vanilla wafer pie·crust. Cool and add Cool Whip.

HOMEMADE VANILLA ICE CREAM

4 qts. milk
2 T. vanilla
6 eggs
A little salt

4T. flour
4 C. sugar
4 C. cream

Put milk in top of double boiler. Add sugar, flour and salt mixed together. Add well beaten eggs. Cook until it coats a spoon. When cool put in freezer and add cream and vanilla and freeze.

BAKED APPLES

1 C. sugar (brown or white)	¼ C. flour
1 C. water	1 tsp. cinnamon
½ C. butter	Baking apples

Butter 9x13-inch pan, fill ¾ full of apples that have been quartered. Mix rest in ingredients and pour over the apples. Bake at 350° for 45 minutes, or until tender.

APRICOT DELIGHT

1 (No. 2½) can apricots
  (drained and strained)
2 T. tapioca

1 C. sugar
1 C. cream (whipped)

Place the juice in top double boiler. Add tapioca, sugar and the strained apricots. Cook 15 minutes. Cool and add whipped cream.

APPLE GOODIE

1 pint apples
Little cinnamon

1 C. sugar

1 stick oleo
½ C. sugar
¼ tsp. salt
½ C. milk

1 C. flour
1 tsp. baking powder
1 C. boiling water

Mix apples, sugar and cinnamon together; let stand. Cream well, oleo and sugar. Add salt, milk, flour and baking powder. Pour batter in pan and spread apples on batter. Pour boiling water on top and bake at 350° until done. Check with toothick. Serve warm.

PINEAPPLE PUDDING CHEESECAKE

1 (8 oz.) pkg. cream cheese
2 C. milk

1 pkg. Jello pineapple cream
 instant pudding
9-inch graham cracker crust

Stir cream cheese until very soft. Blend in ½ C. milk. Add remaining milk and the pudding mix. Beat slowly with egg beater just until well mixed, about 1 minute (do not overbeat). Pour at once into graham crust. Sprinkle graham cracker crumbs lightly over the top. Chill about 1 hour. Serves at least 8 people.

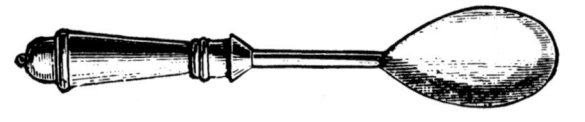

FROZEN PINEAPPLE DESSERT

3 eggs (separated)
Pinch salt
½ C. sugar
8 oz. can crushed pineapple
  (drained)
2 T. lemon juice

1 tsp. vanilla
1 C. heavy cream (whipped)
  (can use Cool Whip)
2 T. sugar
1½ C. vanilla wafers (crushed)

Beat egg yolks, salt and ½ C. sugar. Add pineapple and lemon juice and cook on low heat until it coats a spoon. Add pineapple and cool. Beat egg whites and 2 T. sugar until stiff. Fold them and whipped cream into the custard mixture. Coat the bottom of a 9-inch square pan with wafers, saving some to sprinkle on top of filling. Pour filling on crumbs and freeze. Serves 6-8.

BAKED FRUIT

6 cooked apples or applesauce
1 medium can peaches
1 medium can pears
1 medium can pineapple chunks
Apricots (optional)

1 can cherry pie filling
½ C. brown sugar
1½ tsp. cinnamon
¼ tsp. cloves

Drain all fruit; mix with apples and pie filling. Put in 9x13 inch pan. Mix together brown sugar, cinnamon and cloves; sprinkle over fruit. Bake at 350° for 30 to 45 minutes.

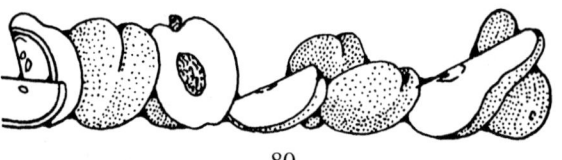

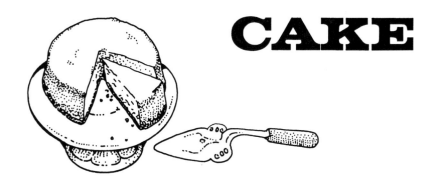

CAKE

SMALL TOWN CAKE

RAISIN CAKE

1 C. raisins
2 C. water
1 stick margarine
1¾ C. flour
1 C. sugar

1 tsp. soda
½ tsp. salt
½ tsp. cinnamon
½ tsp. nutmeg
¼ C. black walnuts (optional)

Boil raisins in water for 10 minutes. Add the margarine; let cool. Mix together flour, sugar, soda, salt, cinnamon and nutmeg. In the same pan, add the flour mxlture to the raisin mixture and stir well. Add nuts, if desired. Pour into greased 8 or 9-inch pan. Bake at 350° for 35 minutes. Frost as desired or serve with whipped topping or ice cream.

RHUBARB CAKE

1½ C. brown or white sugar
½ C. shortening
1 egg
1 tsp. vanilla
1 tsp. soda

1 C. sour cream or buttermilk
2 C. flour
2 C. ½-inch cut rhubarb
½ C. sugar
1 tsp. cinnamon

Cream together sugar, shortening, egg and vanilla. Add soda, buttermilk (or **sour cream**) and flour. Fold in rhubarb. Combine sugar and cinnamon; sprinkle over **top of cake**. Bake in a 9x13-inch pan at 350° for 45 minutes.

PUMPKIN CAKE

1 spice cake mix	3 eggs
1 box instant vanilla pudding	1½ C. can pumpkin
½ C. water	1 tsp. cinnamon
½ C. oil	½ C. pecans

Mix all ingredients together and pour into greased bundt pan. Bake at 350° for 50 to 55 minutes. Let cool.

FROSTING:

¾ stick butter	3 C. powdered sugar
3 oz. cream cheese	1 T. milk

Combine ingredients, mixing well. May use as a frosting or by adding more milk use as a glaze.

STRAWBERRY SHORTCAKE

4 eggs
2 C. sugar
½ tsp. salt
2 tsp. vanilla

2 T. butter
1 C. boiling milk
2 C. flour
2 tsp. baking powder

Beat eggs until very light. Beat in sugar, salt and vanilla. Melt butter in milk. Sift and beat in flour and baking powder. Bake in greased pan 25-30 minutes at 350°. Serve with strawberries and cream.

BANANA CAKE

½ C. butter
1½ C. sugar
2 eggs
½ C. buttermilk
1 C. mashed bananas

½ C. chopped nuts
½ C. chopped dates
2 C. flour
1 tsp. soda
¼ tsp. salt

Cream butter and sugar. Add beaten whole eggs. Beat well. Add milk, bananas, dates and nuts. Sift flour and measure. Add soda and salt and sift again. Add dry ingredients to banana mixture. Bake in round cake pans or 9x13-inch pan. Bake 35 minutes in 350° oven. Use Waldorf Frosting or 7-minute cooked frosting.

APPLESAUCE CAKE

½ C. shortening
1 C. sugar
1 egg
1½ C. flour
1 tsp. soda
1 tsp. salt

1½ tsp. cinnamon
½ tsp. cloves
1 C. hot applesauce
1 C. raisins
1 C. chopped nuts

Cream together shortening, sugar and egg. Add flour, soda, salt, cinnamon **and cloves** alternately with applesauce. Add raisins and nuts. Bake at 350° until **done.**

APPLE CAKE

4 ½ T. butter or oleo
1 ½ C. sugar
1 egg
1 ½ C. flour
1 ½ tsp. soda
1 ½ tsp. vanilla

¾ tsp. salt
4 ½ C. diced apples
½ tsp. cinnamon
½ tsp. nutmeg
½ C. nuts

Cream butter and sugar; add egg. Add flour, soda, salt, spices and vanilla. Fold in apples and nuts. Batter will be very thick. Bake in a 9x13-inch pan at 350° for 35 minutes. Serve with whipped cream or ice cream.

GRANDMA'S CHOCOLATE CAKE

1 C. brown sugar
1 C. white sugar
½ C. shortening
2 eggs
½ C. sour milk (add 2 T. vinegar
  to ½ C. sweet milk to sour it)

2 C. flour
½ tsp. salt
2 tsp. soda
½ C. cocoa
1 C. boiling water

Cream together sugars and shortening. Add eggs and soured milk. Sift together the dry ingredients and add to creamed mixture. Last of all add 1 C. boiling water and mix thoroughly. Bake 45 minutes (pour in a 9x13-inch greased pan - batter will be thin) at 350° or until no dent remains when cake is touched with a finger.

PIE

SMALL TOWN PIE

COCONUT PIE

4 eggs
½ C. flour
2 C. milk (heat to lukewarm)
1¾ C. sugar

¼ C. melted butter
1½ C. coconut
1 tsp. vanilla

Add ingredients in order. Use mixer on medium speed, until well blended. Bake at 350° for 45-50 minutes.

LOW CALORIE CHOCOLATE PIE

1 envelope Knox gelatine
¾ C. sugar or equal substitute
1/8 tsp. salt
1 egg yolk
¾ C. skim milk

3 squares unsweetened chocolate
1 C. ice cold evaporated milk
1 tsp. vanilla
1 baked pie shell

Mix gelatine, sugar and salt. Beat egg yolk and milk together, add to gelatin mixture. Add chocolate. Cook over medium heat, stirring constantly, until chocolate is melted. Do Not Boil. Place pan in bowl of ice water to chill, stirring occasionally, until mixture mounds slightly when dropped from spoon. Fold in beaten evapoarted milk and vanilla or Dream Whip could be used. Pour in shell.

"THAT'S ALL PIE"

1 (6 oz.) frozen lemonade (thawed)   1 can Eagle Brand milk
8 oz. container Cool Whip   Graham cracker crust

Mix together lemonade, Cool Whip and milk. Pour into graham cracker crust and chill for 2 hours.

CHERRY-CREAM CHEESE PIE

1 (9-inch) crumb crust
1 (8 oz.) pkg. cream cheese
1⅓ C. (14 oz. can) Borden's Eagle
   Brand sweetened condensed milk

1 tsp. vanilla
⅓ C. lemon juice
1 can prepared cherry pie filling

Soften cream cheese to room temperature; whip until fluffy. Gradually add Eagle
Brand milk, while continuing to beat until well blended. Add lemon juice and vanilla,
blend well. Pour into crust. Chill 2-3 hours before garnishing top of pie with cherry
pie filling. Double everything except crackers to make a 9x13-inch pan.

DANIEL'S FAVORITE PIE

2 eggs (slightly beaten)
1 (16 oz.) can solid pack pumpkin
¾ C. sugar
½ tsp. salt
1 tsp. ground cinnamon

½ tsp. ground ginger
¼ tsp. ground cloves
1 tsp. pumpkin pie spice
1 (13 oz.) can evaporated milk or
   1⅔ C. Half & Half

Preheat oven to 425°. Combine ingredients in order given. Pour into 9-inch pie shell (with a high edge). Bake for 15 minutes. Reduce temperature to 350° and bake an additional 45 minutes or until knife inserted comes out clean. Cool.

KEY LIME PIE

8 oz. pkg. Cool Whip
1 can Eagle Brand milk

½ C. fresh lime juice
(can use lemon juice)

Beat together well with electric mixer. Pour into graham crust pie shell. Chill well before serving.

RHUBARB PIE

4 C. diced fresh rhubarb　　　2 T. butter
1 C. sugar　　　　　　　　　½ tsp. lemon juice
3 T. minute tapioca

Combine ingredients. Use double crust. Bake at 450° for 15 minutes, then at 350° for 30 minutes.

ANGEL CHIFFON PIE

1⅓ env. unflavored gelatin	⅓ C. sugar
½ C. water	1/8 tsp. salt
1½ C. prepared mincemeat	½ pt. cream (whipped stiff)
3 egg whites	1 (9-inch) baked pie shell (cooled)

Sprinkle gelatin on water in saucepan to soften. Place over low heat until it is soft. Remove from heat and stir in mincemeat. Chill until mixture mounds slightly when dropped from a spoon. Beat egg whites until stiff, gradually add sugar and salt. Beat until very stiff and fold in the gelatin mxiture. Fold in whipped cream and turn into baked shell. Chill until firm. Set baked shell in refrigerator so its cold while gelatin and mincemeat is chilling. I whip cream and egg whites, then mincemeat —is ready.

MAIN DISHES

SMALL TOWN MAIN DISHES

TEXAS HASH

1 lb. ground beef	½ C. uncooked rice
3 large onions (sliced)	2 tsp. salt
1 large green pepper (chopped)	1-2 tsp. chili powder
1 (16 oz.) can tomatoes	1/8 tsp. pepper

In large skillet cook and stir meat, onion and green peppers until meat is brown and vegetables are tender; drain off fat. Stir in tomatoes, rice, salt, chili powder and pepper; heat through. Pour into ungreased 2-quart casserole and bake at 350° for 1 hour.

PIZZA BURGERS

1 lb. hamburger
1 small onion
1 can pizza sauce

1 pkg. hamburger buns
1 pkg. mozzarella cheese

Brown hamburger and onion; pour off grease. Add pizza sauce and simmer. Spoon hamburger on open-faced buns and place cheese on top. Place burgers on cookie sheet and place them under the broiler until cheese starts to melt.

QUICK'N EASY SALMON PATTIES

1 (15 oz.) can salmon
1 egg
⅓ C. minced onion

½ C. flour
1½ tsp. baking powder

Drain salmon, reserving 2 T. of the juice. Mix salmon, egg and onion until sticky. Stir in flour. Add baking powder to salmon juice and stir into salmon mixture. Form into small patties and fry until golden brown (about 5 minutes). Serves 4 to 6.

HAMBALL RECIPE

3 lbs. ground ham
1 lb. hamburger
1 lb. ground pork
3 C. graham crackers (crushed)
3 eggs

2 C. milk
1 tsp. onion salt
1 tsp. salt
1 tsp. liquid smoke
¼ tsp. pepper

SAUCE:
1 can cond. tomato soup
½ can water
1 C. brown sugar

1 T. dry mustard
¼ C. vinegar

Each hamball is to contain ½ C. of meat mixture to make 24. Put sauce over balls before baking. Bake at 325° for 1 hour.

CROCK POT ITALIAN BEEF

½ tsp. red pepper
1 tsp. garlic
1 tsp. onion powder
2 tsp. salt
1 tsp. pepper
Beef roast

1 tsp. oregano
2 tsp. parsley
2 tsp. sweet basil
2 bay leaves
3 C. water

Trim fat from beef roast. Place all the above in crock pot. Cook on low heat all day. Serve as dip sandwiches.

MEATZZA *(Rangetop Skillet Meat Loaf)*

1½ lbs. ground beef
1 tsp. salt
½ tsp. pepper
1 tsp. Italian seasoning
1½ tsp. dry mustard
2 tsp. minced insant onion

½ tsp. minced instant garlic
1 egg
½ C. fine dry bread crumbs
1 scant C. pizza sauce
4 oz. grated or sliced mozzarella cheese

Mix together first 9 ingredients and ½ pizza sauce. Pat mixture in 10-inch skillet. Pour remaining sauce over meat and spread to 1-inch from edge. Cook covered, over low heat for 20 minutes. Continue cooking, uncovered over moderate heat another 20 minues. Drain and arrange cheese over meat, cover and let stand off heat until cheese melts. Makes 4 to 6 servings.

FIVE CAN CASSEROLE *(Chicken)*

2 C. boned & diced chicken
1 can chicken noodle soup
1 can cream of chicken soup
1 small can evaporated milk

1 (3 oz.) can Chow Mein noodles
½ C. melted margarine
4 slices diced bread

Combine the first 5 ingredients. Place in square or small rectangular dish. Toss bread crumbs in melted butter. Arrange on top of casserole. Bake for 35 to 45 minutes until bubbly and bread is nicely browned. Freezes nicely before baked.

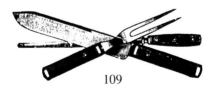

MAKE AHEAD CHICKEN CASSEROLE

2 C. small shell or elbow macaroni	½ C. celery
3 C. cubed chicken	1 onion
2 (10¼ oz. ea.) cans mushroom soup	½ small jar pimento
2½ C. broth	Salt & pepper
1 C. grated Velveeta cheese	Crushed potato chips

Put macaroni in greased 9x13-inch pan. Add 3 C. diced chicken evenly over macaroni. Add celery, onion, pimento, salt and pepper. Add soup and broth, mixed together. Put cheese over the top. Cover and refrigerate overnight. Top with crushed potato chips just before baking. Bake, uncovered at 350° for 1 hour. Leftovers can be frozen.

BARBEQUED BEEF

1½ bottles ketchup (32 oz. size)
Spinkle of garlic salt
1 T. tobasco sauce
Sprinkle of red pepper
3 T. chopped celery

4 T. brown sugar
2 chopped onions
1 tsp. liquid smoke
Black pepper, to taste
3-4 lb. roast

Mix all ingredients together. Cook a 3-4 lb. roast and let cool. Pull meat apart. Pour in barbeque sauce and simmer in oven or crock pot. Makes great sandwiches!

MOCK SIRLOIN

2 lbs. lean ground beef	1 C. cracker crumbs
2 tsp. salt	¼ tsp. pepper
1 tsp. prepared mustard	⅓ C. catsup
⅓ C. evaporated milk	1 egg

Mix together and place on foil on broiler pan; pat mixture into shape of a sirloin steak, 1 to 1½-inch thick. Brush with soft butter. Broil 4-inches from heat for 15 to 20 minutes or until desired doneness. Do not turn. Serve with lemon butter made with 3 T. melted butter, juice of ½ lemon, 1 T. Worcestershire sauce and chopped parsley. Makes 8 servings.

BARBECUED HAM BALLS

1¼ lbs. ground ham
1¼ lbs. hamburger
2 eggs

1 C. crushed graham cracker
1 C. milk

SAUCE:
1 can tomato soup
1¼ C. brown sugar

1 tsp. dry mustard
⅔ C. vinegar

Place meatballs in a large cake pan. Combine the sauce ingredients and pour over meatballs. Serves 10 to 12. Bake at 375° for 1½ hours.

SALMON LOAF

1 egg	½ tsp. salt
2 C. salmon & liquid (prefer pink)	1/8 tsp. pepper
1 C. grated cheese (Velveeta)	1 T. grated onion
1 C. soft bread crumbs	1 T. melted butter

Beat egg in bowl. Add salmon which has been cleaned and broken into large chunks, no smaller than a whole walnut. (I remove bones, skin and dark pieces of salmon.) Add rest of ingredients and mix with your hands, being careful not to break up the salmon pieces. Bake, covered in a buttered casserole. In order to keep loaf from getting crusty, place casserole in a pan of water while it is baking for 1 hour at 350°.

BAKED CHICKEN

½ pt. commercial sour cream
2 T. lemon juice
2 tsp. Worcestershire sauce
1 tsp. celery salt
1 tsp. paprika

½ tsp. garlic salt
¼ tsp. salt and pepper
3 lbs. frying chicken (cut up)
1 pkg. herb seasoned stuffing
   rolled to fine crumbs
Melted butter

Mix together sour cream, juice, sauce, dry seasonings. Dip chicken pieces in this mixture and roll in stuffing crumbs. Arrange pieces in shallow greased dish. Brush with melted butter. Place uncovered in 350° oven for 1 hour or until tender and crusty brown.

LONDON BROIL

2 lbs. round steak
⅓ C. soy sauce
2 T. salad oil
1 T. molasses

1 tsp. ginger
1 tsp. dry mustard
3 cloves garlic or powder

Place steak in covered glass dish. Combine ingredients. Pour over steak and turn to coat. Marinate, turning occasionally for 4-6 hours. Broil.

BARBECUED MEATBALLS

13 oz. can evaporated milk
3 lbs. hamburger
2 C. oatmeal
2 eggs
1 C. chopped onion

½ tsp. garlic
2 tsp. salt
½ tsp. pepper
2 tsp. chili powder

SAUCE:
2 C. catsup
1 C. brown sugar
2 T. liquid smoke

½ tsp. garlic
½ C. onion (optional)

Mix and shape into balls. (I make large ones for a meal, small if for cocktail.) Put in pans in one layer.

For Sauce: Mix sauce until sugar dissolves. Pour over meatballs and bake at 325° for 1 hour. Can be made and frozen. Thaw and bake as usual.

SUPER SHELLS

36 jumbo shells
  (cooked according to box)
2 lbs. browned hamburger
Onion, to taste
1 lb. cottage cheese

1 (8 oz.) pkg. shredded cheddar
  cheese
1 (8 oz.) pkg. mozzarella cheese
½ C. Hellman's mayonnaise
1 super size jar spaghetti sauce

Place small amount of sauce in bottom of large baking pan. Pack mixture tightly into cooked shells and place in baking pan. Pour remaining spaghetti sauce over shells, making sure sauce gets down between shells to coat. Sprinkle a little parmesan cheese on top. Cover with foil and place in refrigerator overnight. Bake at 350° for 30 to 40 minutes or until bubbly.

TUNA CASSEROLE

1 can cream of mushroom soup
1 can tuna
1 can peas

½ C. milk
1 small bag of potato chips

Put ½ of the chips in the above mixture and put the rest on top. Bake at 350° for 20 minutes.

HAMBURGER AND TATER TOT CASSEROLE

1 lb. hamburger
Tater tots
1 can cream of mushroom soup

Salt & pepper, to taste
Potato chips

Press hamburger into bottom of 9x9-inch baking dish. Salt and pepper, to taste. Pour 1 can mushroom soup over meat. Place frozen tater tots over soup mixture. Top with potato chips and bake at 350° for 1 hour.

HAMBURGER PIE

1 lb. hamburger
½ C. onion
1 (15½ oz.) can green beans (drained)
1 (10¾ oz.) can tomato soup
¼ C. water
¼ C. water

¾ tsp. salt
1/8 tsp. pepper
3 med. potatoes (mashed with milk)
1 egg (beaten)
½ C. shredded American cheese

Brown hamburger with onion. Put beans, soup and hamburger in casserole; top with whipped potatoes. (Add egg to the potatoes when you mash them.) Bake, uncovered in 1½-quart casserole at 350° for 25 to 30 minutes.

MOTHER'S BAKED OYSTERS

1 pt. oysters
1 ¼ C. cracker crumbs
1 ½ tsp. salt
Dash of pepper

⅓ C. butter (oleo)
1 beaten egg
1 T. water

Wash, examine and drain oysters. Mix salt and pepper with crumbs. Add to melted butter. Dip oysters in crumbs, then into egg and water mixture and again into crumbs. Spread on a buttered glass baking dish (one layer only). Dot with butter or crumbled cooked bacon. Bake at 375° for 15 to 20 minutes. Enjoy!

TUNA CASSEROLE

1 medium onion
2 stalks celery (diced)
2 (9 oz. ea.) cans tuna
1 can mushroom soup
¾ C. milk
8 oz. Velveeta cheese

8 oz. Velveeta cheese
½ C. sharp cheese
¼ C. sliced olives
¼ C. sour cream
4 C. cooked noodles

Brown onions and celery. Add tuna, soup and milk. Cook until blended. Add cheese and sour cream; cook until melted. Add noodles and olives. Bake at 350° for 30 minutes. Substitute: Good with cubed turkey or chicken rather than tuna.

MEXICAN CHILI CASSEROLE

3 C. large Frito corn chips
1 large chopped onion
1 lb. ground beef
1 (16 oz.) can red kidney beans
1 large can tomatoes (cut-up)

1 C. shredded cheddar cheese (mild)
1 (8 oz.) can tomato sauce
1½ tsp. chili powder
1 tsp. salt
Black olives

Mix kidney beans, tomatoes, tomato sauce, chili powder and salt. Saute onion and ground beef until tender. In casserole, line bottom with corn chips, then put layer of onions and ground beef, a layer of chili mixture, then cheese. Repeat and top with cheese and black olive halves. Bake for 1 hour in 4-quart casserole at 350°. Serves 8.

WILD RICE CASSEROLE

1 C. wild rice (uncooked)
1 can cream of mushroom soup
1 can milk

1 can onion soup (Campbells)
1 can water

Wash and soak wild rice for several hours. Mix rice with all ingredients into casserole dish. Cook for 2 hours or until done at 325°. Good with chicken or turkey.

CHICKEN SUPREME

1 pkg. uncooked macaroni
1 pt. milk (may use chicken broth)
2 cans mushroom soup
1 small onion (chopped)

½ lb. Velveeta cheese
4 hard boiled eggs
2½ C. cooked chicken
1 small can mushrooms

Combine all ingredients and let set in refrigerator overnight. Bake in a 9x13½-inch pan for 1 hour at 350°.

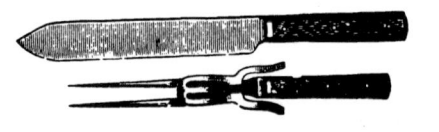

BAKED CHICKEN WITH RICE

1 cut up fryer
1 C. uncooked minute rice
1 can mushroom soup

1 can cream of chicken soup
1 can water

Mix rice, soups and water in an oblong baking dish. Place chicken pieces on top of this mixture and season with salt and pepper. Bake at 350° about 1½ hours. Serves 5-6.

CHICKEN CASSEROLE

2 C. cooked and diced chicken	1 C. chicken broth
1 C. chopped celery	1 C. water
½ C. chopped onion	1 C. uncooked rice
1 can mushroom soup	1 T. soy sauce

Brown onion and celery in butter. Mix all ingredients. Bake 1½ hours at 350° or until rice is done.

GROUND BEEF CASSEROLE

2 C. macaroni (cooked)
1 C. mozzarella cheese
1 lb. lean ground beef

10 oz. pkg. frozen vegetables
8 oz. can tomato sauce
Salt & pepper

Preheat oven to 350°. Grease 2-quart casserole. Brown ground beef and drain off fat. Combine beef with vegetables, macaroni and tomato sauce; season to taste. **Pour** into casserole and top with cheese. Cover and bake for 35 minutes.

HAMBURGER ORIENTAL

1 lb. hamburger
4 onions
6 beef bouillon cubes

1 head cabbage (chopped)
6 T. cooking oil
1 T. curry powder
Salt to taste

Saute onions in oil, add bouillon. Cook for 2-3 minutes. Add cabbage, cook 10-15 minutes. Brown meat with curry powder. Drain fat, and add meat to the cabbage mixture. Mix well and serve.

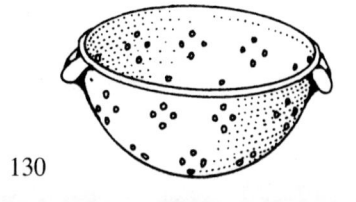

6 CAN CASSEROLE

1 can cream of chicken soup
1 can chicken with rice soup
1 can cream of celery soup

1 can evaporated milk
1 large can Chinese noodles
2-3 cans boned chicken

Mix together and put in 9x13-inch pan. Top with crushed potato chips and bake at 350° until bubbly.

EASY TURKEY/CHICKEN A LA KING

¼ C. finely chopped onion
¼ C. margarine or butter
2 C. milk
2 (10½ oz. ea.) cans cream of
　chicken soup

10 oz. pkg. frozen peas
2 C. cubed cooked turkey or chicken
2 T. chopped pimento
¼ tsp. pepper

In large saucepan, cook onion in margarine over medium heat until tender. Stir in milk, soup and peas; bring to boil, stirring constantly. Cook over medium heat, stirring occasionally for 5 minutes. Stir in turkey or chicken, pimento and pepper; cook until heated through. Serve over egg noodles, toast or refrigerated biscuits.

HAM BALLS

2½ lbs. ground ham
2 lbs. ground pork
1 lb. ground beef

3 C. crushed graham cracker
2 C. milk
3 eggs

SAUCE:
2 cans tomato soup
½ C. vinegar

2½ C. brown sugar
2 tsp. dry mustard

Mix first 6 ingredients well and form into balls (walnut size). Place in large pan at least 9x13-inch and cover with topping. (May wish to place in 2 pans.) Bake at 300° for 1½ hours.

CHINESES STYLE RIBS

4 lbs. pork ribs country style

MARINADE:

4 T. vegetable oil	Salt & pepper
1 C. finely chopped onion	1 C. beef consome'
½ C. finely chopped green pepper	¼ C. vinegar
1 clove of garlic	½ C. brown sugar

Put ribs in kettle, cover with water, bring to boil and simmer for approximately 1 hour. Place cooked ribs in non-metal container and cover with marinade for several hours or overnight. Turn several times. Make marinade by heating oil and adding onions, pepper and garlic. Stir in consome', vinegar and brown sugar; simmer approximately 30 minutes. Grill ribs over medium hot coals, turning often and basting as necessary to crisp and brown ribs.

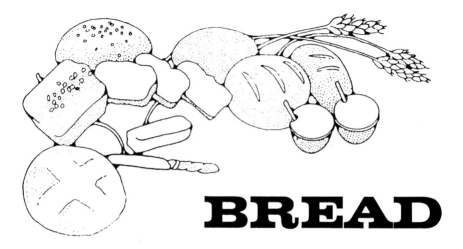

BREAD

SMALL TOWN BREAD

BANANA NUT BREAD

½ C. softened butter or margarine
1 C. well-packed brown sugar
1 egg
3 T. milk, orange or apple juice
1 C. ripe mashed bananas
2 C. whole-wheat flour

2½ tsp. baking powder
¼ tsp. salt
½ C. nuts
1 tsp. vanilla
¼ tsp. almond flavoring
½ C. flake coconut

Cream butter or margarine and brown sugar. Add vanilla and almond flavorings; beat in egg. Stir together flour, baking powder and salt. Add liquid and bananas to creamed mixture. Stir in flour, add nuts and coconut. Pour in two greased and floured loaf pans (approximately 8x4x2½-inches). Bake at 350° for 50 to 60 minutes or until bread pulls away from pan.

CARROT BREAD

1 C. sugar
¾ C. oil
2 eggs
1½ C. flour

1 tsp. baking powder
1 tsp. cinnamon
¼ tsp. salt
1½ C. shredded carrots

Mix and bake at 350° for 1 hour.

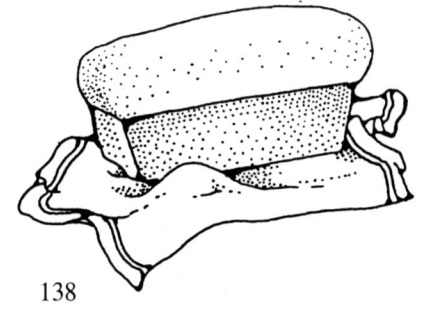

138

"HOT STUFF" BREAD

2 heaping tsp. minced Jalapeno chiles
1 C. grated Tillamook cheese
  (colby will do)
4 tsp. dry yeast

1 tsp. salt
2 tsp. sugar
2 C. very warm tap water
6 C. all-purpose flour

EGG WASH:
1 egg

½ C. water

Mix all ingredients. Knead until barely sticky. Put in greased bowl and cover. Let rise for 30 minutes. Punch down. Roll out in 18x12-inch rectangle. Cut into strips 1½x6-inches. Roll up each strip like a cinnamon roll. Place end of roll on baking pan like snail sitting up. Brush with egg wash. Let rise 10 minutes. Bake at 350° for 30 minutes or until golden brown.

COTTAGE CHEESE ROLLS

2 pkgs. dry yeast
⅓ C. warm water
1½ C. cottage cheese
½ C. shortening
1 egg

3½ C. flour
⅓ C. sugar
2 tsp. salt
½ tsp. soda

Combine yeast, water and ½ of sugar; let stand for 5 minutes. Beat cottage cheese, egg and melted shortening until well blended. Add yeast mixture. Add dry ingredients and knead for 10 minutes (dough will be soft). Let rise until double in size. Pat down and let rest for 10 minutes. Shape rolls and let rise until almost double in size. Bake at 375° for 15 minutes.

GRAHAM ROLLS

2 C. lukewarm milk
½ C. sugar
2 tsp. salt
2 pkgs. yeast, dissolved in
  ½ C. lukewarm water

2 C. graham flour
5-5½ C. sifted flour
2 eggs
½ C. shortening

Mix milk, sugar and salt. Add 2 pkgs. yeast, dissolved in lukewarm water. Add eggs, shortening and graham flour. Beat well and add sifted flour. Knead until smooth and elastic. Place in greased bowl and let rise until double; punch down. After second rising, shape dough in desired rolls. Let rise for 15 to 20 minutes. Bake at 350° for 20 minutes.

PUMPKIN BREAD

3 ½ C. flour
2 tsp. soda
1 ½ tsp. salt
1 tsp. cinnamon
1 tsp. nutmeg
3 C. sugar

1 C. oil
4 large eggs or 5 medium
⅔ C. water
2 C. pumpkin (1 small can)
½ C. nutmeats (optional)

Mix all dry ingredients into large bowl. Make a well and add remaining ingredients. Mix until smooth and bake at 325°. Time varies as to size of pans. Three loaf pans, about 1 hour. Smaller pans are less time.

ZUCCHINI BREAD

4 eggs	1 ½ tsp. salt
2 C. sugar	1 ½ tsp. baking soda
1 C. oil	1 tsp. cinnamon
3 ½ C. flour	¾ tsp. baking powder
2 C. grated zucchini	1 tsp. vanilla

Beat the eggs in mixing bowl. Beat in sugar and oil. Combine dry ingredients and add to egg mixture. Add zucchini and vanilla. Stir well. Grease and flour two loaf pans. Bake at 350° for 55 minutes. May glaze with a powdered sugar glaze.

BUTTER HORN ROLLS

1 cake compressed yeast	3 eggs
1 C. sweet milk	½ tsp. salt
½ C. sugar	4 C. flour
½ C. butter	

In a large mixing bowl, place one compressed yeast cake and crumble it with one teaspoon sugar until it becomes liquid. Add milk, heated to lukewarm, a scant ½ C. sugar, soft butter, eggs (well-beaten), salt, enough flour for a soft dough, stiff enough to knead. Let stand overnight. In the morning place the dough on a bread board, knead it a little and cut in half. Roll each piece as round as possible and about ¼-inch thick, like a large pie crust. Cut each into 16 pie-shaped pieces, beginning at the broad end of each piece, roll it toward small end. Put rolls on buttered tins and set aside to rise. Bake at 350° for 20 mintues.

DUMPLINGS

1 egg
¾ C. milk
2 C. flour

3 tsp. baking powder
½ tsp. salt
1 T. melted butter

Mix egg, milk, flour, baking powder and salt well, then add melted butter. Drop by spoonsful in boiling chicken broth. Cover and boil slowly for 10 minutes. Do not raise the lid.

PUMPKIN BREAD

½ C. vegetable oil (Crisco)
2 eggs (beaten)
1 C. pumpkin
⅓ C. water
1 ¾ C. sifted flour
¾ tsp. salt

½ tsp. nutmeg
1 ½ C. sugar
½ tsp. cinnamon
1 tsp. baking soda
¼ C. raisins
¼ C. pecans or walnuts

Combine oil, eggs, water and pumpkin. Sift dry ingredients into bowl. Pour in liquid and blend thoroughly. Stir in raisins and pecans. Bake at 350° for 1 hour in a generously greased loaf pan.

CANDY

SMALL TOWN CANDY

JOYCE'S GOODIES

6 oz. pkg. chocolate chips	1 stick oleo
½ C. peanut butter	8 C. rice chex
1 C. powdered sugar	

Melt chocolate chips, peanut butter and butter together. Pour over rice chex. Shake in paper sack with 1 C. powdered sugar.

NUTRITIOUS CANDY

½ C. peanut butter
½ C. honey
½ C. powdered milk

1 T. wheat germ
Coconut shreds, chopped nuts or
    sesame seeds (optional)

Mix peanut butter with honey. Add powdered milk (more as needed to form a stiff dough). Spread out on waxed paper and knead wheat germ into mixture. Roll into a log, wrap in wax paper and chill for at least one hour. Slice to serve or can be rolled into balls and rolled in coconut shreds, chopped nuts or sesame seeds.

PRALINES

2 C. sugar	Pinch of salt
1 tsp. soda	2 T. butter
1 C. buttermilk	2 C. pecan halves

In a large kettle combine sugar, soda, salt and buttermilk. Cook over high heat for 5 minutes or to 210°, stirring constantly. Add butter and pecans; cook for 5 minutes longer until hard ball stage (230°) and cool about 5 minutes. Beat until creamy and drop by spoon on waxed paper or put into a pan and cut it while warm.

ALMOND ROCA

1 C. butter
1 C. sugar
12 oz. Hershey Milk Chocolate
  (bars, broken or chips)

6 oz. almonds
  (sliced or chopped into chunks)

Melt butter, add sugar and turn to high heat. Stir with a wooden spoon until mixture boils. Continue cooking and stirring until mixture turns tan color. Stir in 3 oz. of almonds. Pour into buttered 9x13-inch pan or jelly roll pan. Sprinkle chocolates on top and spread as melting. Add rest of almonds, pressing lightly into the chocolate. Cool for 1 hour in the refrigerator. Break into pieces. Makes 2 lbs.

BROKEN GLASS CANDY

2 C. white sugar
½ C. water
1 C. white Karo

½ to 1 tsp. food coloring
½ tsp. cinnamon oil

Cook to hard crack (stir once in awhile). Turn off heat and add ½ tsp. cinnamon oil and stir. (Do not lean over pan while doing this.) Pour into well-buttered pan and let cool. Remove from pan and put in plastic bag and break into pieces.

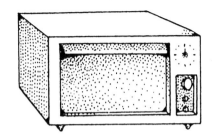

MICROWAVE

SMALL TOWN MICROWAVE

MICROWAVE MEAT LOAF

1 ½ lbs. ground beef
½ C. bread crumbs
1 egg (beaten)
¾ C. milk

¼ C. finely chopped onion
1 ½ tsp. salt (seasoned salt)
¼ tsp. pepper
½ C. ketchup

Mix well in a bowl, everything except ketchup. Pack lightly into pie dish. Cover with waxed paper and cook for 5 minutes at Medium. Top with ketchup. Cook, covered for an additional 10 to 15 minues on High. It will cook faster in pie dish. If using temperature probe, it should reach 160°. Remove from oven, cover with foil and let stand for 5 minutes. Serves 6.

MICROWAVE PIZZA CASSEROLE

½ bag egg noodles
½ lb. hamburger
½ lb. sausage
16 oz. jar pizza sauce

Pizza relishes: Onion,
    mushrooms, green pepper, etc.
2 C. shredded mozzarella cheese

Cook noodles in boiling water for 3 minutes. Place in 9x13-inch glass dish. Brown hamburger and sausage; drain. Place over noodles. Cover with pizza relishes, then cover with pizza sauce. Cook for 15 minutes on High. Add shredded mozzarella cheese. Cook 10 minutes more on High.

NEED GIFTS?

Are you up a stump for some nice gifts for some nice people in your life? Here's a list of some great cookbooks. Just check 'em off, stick a check in an envelope with these pages, and we'll get your books off to you. Add $3.00 for shipping and handling for the first book and then $.50 cents more for each additional one. If you order over $50.00, forget the shipping and handling.

Mini Cookbooks
(Only 3 1/2 x 5) With Maxi Good Eatin' - 160 or 176 pages - $5.95

- ❑ Alabama Cooking
- ❑ Arizona Cooking
- ❑ Arkansas Cooking
- ❑ Dakota Cooking
- ❑ Dixie Cooking
- ❑ Georgia Cooking
- ❑ Illinois Cooking
- ❑ Indiana Cooking
- ❑ Iowa Cookin'
- ❑ Kansas Cookin'
- ❑ Kentucky Cookin'
- ❑ Michigan Cooking
- ❑ Minnesota Cookin'
- ❑ Missouri Cookin'
- ❑ New Jersey Cooking
- ❑ New Mexico Cooking
- ❑ New York Cooking
- ❑ North Carolina Cooking
- ❑ Ohio Cooking
- ❑ Pennsylvania Cooking

- ❑ South Carolina Cooking
- ❑ Tennessee Cooking
- ❑ Virginia Cooking
- ❑ Wisconsin Cooking
- ❑ Amish-Mennonite Apple Cookbook
- ❑ Amish-Mennonite Berry Cookbook
- ❑ Amish-Mennonite Peach Cookbook
- ❑ Amish-Mennonite Pumpkin Cookbook
- ❑ Amish & Mennonite Strawberry Cookbook
- ❑ Apples! Apples! Apples!
- ❑ Apples Galore
- ❑ Basil A-Z
- ❑ Berries! Berries! Berries!
- ❑ Berries Galore!
- ❑ Blueberry Blues Cookbook
- ❑ Bountiful Blueberries
- ❑ Cherries! Cherries! Cherries!
- ❑ Cherries Galore
- ❑ Citrus! Citrus! Citrus!

- ❑ Cooking Seafood & Poultry with Wine
- ❑ Cooking with Asparagus
- ❑ Cooking with Cider
- ❑ Cooking with Garlic
- ❑ Cooking with Spirits
- ❑ Cooking with Sweet Onions
- ❑ Cooking with Wine
- ❑ Cooking with Things Go Baa
- ❑ Cooking with Things Go Cluck
- ❑ Cooking with Things Go Moo
- ❑ Cooking with Things Go Oink
- ❑ Cooking with Things Go Splash
- ❑ CSA Cookbook ($4.95)
- ❑ Crazy for Basil
- ❑ Crockpot Cookbook
- ❑ Dixie Cookbook
- ❑ Good Cookin' From the Plain People
- ❑ Herbs! Herbs! Herbs!
- ❑ How to Make Salsa
- ❑ Kid Cookin'

($5.95 continued)

- ☐ Kid Fun
- ☐ Kid Money
- ☐ Kid Pumpkin Fun Book
- ☐ Midwest Small Town Cookin'
- ☐ Muffins Cookbook (Veggies, Fruit, Nut)
- ☐ Nuts! Nuts! Nuts!
- ☐ Off To College Cookbook
- ☐ Peaches! Peaches! Peaches!
- ☐ Pecans! Pecans! Pecans!
- ☐ Pumpkins! Pumpkins! Pumpkins!
- ☐ Recipes for Appetizers & Beverages Using Wine
- ☐ Recipes for Desserts Using Wine
- ☐ Some Like It Hot
- ☐ Soup's On!
- ☐ Southwest Cooking
- ☐ Super Simple Cookin'
- ☐ To Take the *Gamey* out of the Game Cookbook
- ☐ Wild Rice Cookbook
- ☐ Working Girl Cookbook

Larger Mini Cookbooks
176 - 204 pages - $6.95

- ☐ Cooking with Mulling Spices
- ☐ Grass-Fed Beef Recipes
- ☐ The Grilling & BBQ Cookbook

($6.95 continued)

- ☐ Holiday & Get-Together Cookbook
- ☐ Veggie Talk Coloring & Story Book
- ☐ Winter Squash Cookbook
- ☐ The Zero Calorie Chocolate Cookbook

In-Between Cookbooks
(5 1/2 x 8 1/2) - 150 pages - $9.95

- ☐ Adaptable Apple Cookbook
- ☐ Amish Ladies Cookbook - Old Husbands
- ☐ Amish Ladies Cookbook - Young Husbands
- ☐ Amish Ladies Carry-To-The-Field Cold Lunches Cookbook
- ☐ An Apple A Day Cookbook
- ☐ Baseball Moms' Cookbook
- ☐ Basketball Moms' Cookbook
- ☐ Bird Up! Pheasant Cookbook
- ☐ Buffalo Cookbook
- ☐ Camp Cookin'
- ☐ Catfish Cookin' Cookbook
- ☐ Civil War Cookin', Stories, 'n Such
- ☐ Cookin' Panfish Cookbook
- ☐ Cooking Ala Nude
- ☐ Cooking for a Crowd
- ☐ Cooking Up Some Winners Cookbook

($9.95 continued)

- ☐ Cooking with Beer
- ☐ Cooking with Moonshine
- ☐ Country Cooking Recipes from my Amish Heritage
- ☐ Das Hausbarn Cookbook
- ☐ Eating Ohio
- ☐ Farmers Market Cookbook
- ☐ Feast of Moons Indian Cookbook
- ☐ Funky Duck Cookbook
- ☐ Halloween Fun Book
- ☐ Herbal Cookery
- ☐ Hunting in the Nude Cookbook
- ☐ Indian Cooking Cookbook
- ☐ Japanese Cooking
- ☐ Keep The Skinny Kid Skinny Cookbook
- ☐ Kids' No-Cook Cookbook
- ☐ Mad About Garlic
- ☐ Mormon Trail Cookbook
- ☐ New Cooks' Cookbook
- ☐ No-Stove, No-Sharp Knife Kids' Cookbook
- ☐ Off the Farm, Out of the Garden Cookbook
- ☐ Outdoor Cooking for Outdoor Men
- ☐ Plantation Cookin' Cookbook
- ☐ Pumpkin Patch, Proverbs & Pies

($9.95 continued)

- ❏ Shhh Cookbook
- ❏ Soccer Mom's Cookbook
- ❏ Southwest Ghost Town Cookbook
- ❏ Southwest Native American Cookbook
- ❏ Southwest Vegetarian Cookbook
- ❏ Trailer Trash Cookbook
- ❏ Turn of the Century Cooking
- ❏ Vegan Vegetarian Cookbook
- ❏ Venison Cookbook
- ❏ Vittles Fixin's Cookbook
- ❏ Western Frontier Cookbook

Biggie Cookbooks
(5 1/2 x 8 1/2) - 200 plus pages - $11.95

- ❏ Aphrodisiac Cooking

- ❏ Barn Raising & Threshers Cookbook
- ❏ Bride's Guide (1910) to the Culinary Arts Cookbook
- ❏ Buy Fresh, Buy Local Cookbook
- ❏ Covered Bridges Cookbook
- ❏ Depression Times Cookbook
- ❏ Dial-a-Dream Cookbook
- ❏ Discover the Phillipines Cookbook
- ❏ Flat Out, Dirt Cheap Cookin'
- ❏ Grandma's Cookbook
- ❏ Grits Shall Rise Again
- ❏ Have You Considered Cooking
- ❏ Hormone Helper Cookbook
- ❏ I-Got-Funner-Things-To Do Cookbook
- ❏ Le Ricette (Italian) Cookbook

($11.95 continued)

- ❏ Little "Ol Blue Haired Church Lady Cookbook
- ❏ Lumber Camp & Saw Milling Cookbook
- ❏ Mississippi River Cookbook
- ❏ Quilters' Cookbook
- ❏ Real Men Cook on Sunday Cookbook
- ❏ Southern Homemade Cooking
- ❏ Spice 'N Wine Cookbook
- ❏ Taste of Las Vegas Cookbook
- ❏ Vegetarian Wild Game Cookbook
- ❏ Victorian Sunday Dinners
- ❏ Wild Critter Cookbook

HEARTS 'N TUMMIES COOKBOOK CO.
3544 Blakslee St. • Wever, Iowa 52658
1-800-571-2665

Name _____

Address _____

_____ Ph.# _____

*You Iowa folks gotta kick in another 6% for Sales Tax.